EARTH

A TRUE BOOK

by

Larry Dane Brimner

Children's Press®
A Division of Grolier Publishing
New York London Hong Kong Sydney
Danbury, Connecticut

Earth's oceans help control the temperature of the planet.

Subject Consultant
Peter Goodwin
Science Department Chairman
Kent School, Kent, CT

Reading Consultant
Linda Cornwell
Learning Resource Consultant
Indiana Department
of Education

Author's Dedication:
For my friends at
Settlers Way
Elementary School

Library of Congress Cataloging-in-Publication Data

Brimner, Larry Dane.
 Earth / by Larry Dane Brimner.
  p.   cm. — (A true book)
 Includes bibliographical references and index.
 Summary: Describes the planet Earth, exploring its composition, early
ideas about its shape and position in the solar system, current theories
about its creation, and its important relationship with the moon.
  ISBN 0-516-20620-6 (lib. bdg.)   0-516-26431-1 (pbk.)
  1. Earth—Juvenile literature. [1. Earth] I. Title. II. Series.
QB631.4.B75   1998
550—dc21

                                                97-48867
                                                    CIP
                                                     AC

Contents

The Solar System

Venus

Moon

Earth

Asteroid Belt

Saturn

Neptune

Our Home

Earth is one of the nine planets in our solar system. It is the only one you can explore without rocketing into space. All you need to do is open your door. Earth's surface lies just outside. Earth's atmosphere, or the gases that surround Earth, is the air you breathe.

**Earth is the third planet
from the Sun.**

We know a lot about Earth, because it is where we live, work, and play.

Since Earth is our home, we know a lot about it. But even so, there is a lot more that scientists would like to learn. Most of Earth's secrets are hidden deep beneath its surface.

Early Ideas

Today, we think of Earth differently than people who lived long ago. In very early times, some people thought Earth was a hollow mountain surrounded by a huge ocean. Above this mountain was a solid roof that contained the Sun, the Moon, and the stars.

Ancient people living in the Middle East thought Earth was a hollow mountain surrounded by ocean.

The Greeks and Egyptians who lived thousands of years ago figured out that Earth is a ball-shaped globe. But many Europeans living just five hundred years ago believed that

The Greeks knew Earth was round, as can be seen in this sculpture (above). An early map of Earth (right) shows Africa, Europe, and Asia.

the Earth was flat. They "proved" this idea by pointing to maps that were drawn on flat cloth!

Early astronomers also figured out that Earth and all the planets orbit, or travel around, the Sun. Today, we know that Earth orbits the Sun at an amazing 67,000 miles per hour (108,000 kilometers per hour)! At that speed, it takes 365 days, or one year, to travel around the Sun once. Earth's orbit is an elliptical path, similar to a stretched-out circle. Earth is about 93 million miles (150 million km) from the Sun.

An early view of the planets orbiting the Sun

We also know that Earth rotates, or spins, as it orbits the Sun. It is daytime on the side facing the Sun and night-time on the side away from the Sun. Earth's rotation takes 24 hours, or one day.

The Beginning

Most scientists think Earth and the other planets formed about 4.5 billion years ago from a swirling cloud of gases and dust. As the cloud spun around the Sun, the dust particles bumped into one another and got very hot. Sometimes, the particles stuck together

The planets grew bigger and bigger as they swirled around the Sun.

and formed large objects, such as Earth.

Over millions of years, the outer layer of Earth cooled to form a thin crust. Underneath the crust, the hot rocks made

Steam erupted from beneath Earth's crust and formed the oceans.

steam. The steam erupted through cracks in the crust, creating the first atmosphere. Then the steam fell back to Earth as rain and eventually covered the planet with oceans.

Scientists think Earth's first atmosphere was mostly carbon dioxide. This is the gas plants need to live. So simple plants began to appear. These plants produced so much oxygen that Earth's atmosphere began to change, and new creatures

Plants are important to life on Earth. They produce oxygen, which people need to live.

began to appear. Today, millions of different plants and animals live on Earth.

Earth is a very special place. As far as we know, it is the only planet that can support living things.

On the Move

When the oceans formed, Earth's higher land areas stayed above water. Most scientists agree that Earth had only one land mass about 250 million years ago. Alfred Wegener (1880–1930), a German meteorologist (a scientist who studies the atmosphere), named this

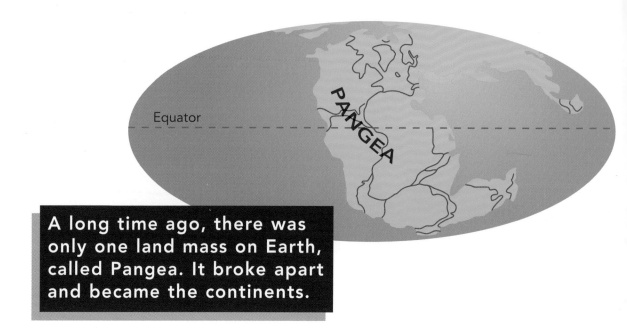

Equator

PANGEA

A long time ago, there was only one land mass on Earth, called Pangea. It broke apart and became the continents.

land mass Pangea. Wegener and others believed that the land mass broke apart into several pieces of land. We call these pieces continents.

That idea gained support in the 1960s when scientists discovered that Earth's crust is not one solid piece. Instead, it is split into pieces called plates. The plates move constantly because they float on a layer of hot, liquid rock. As far as we know, Earth is the only planet that has moving plates.

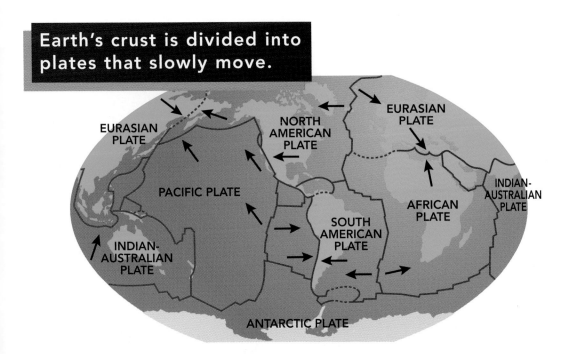

Earth's crust is divided into plates that slowly move.

Shake, Rattle, and Quake!

We don't usually feel Earth's plates moving. This is because they move slowly—only about 1 to 7 inches (2.5 to 18 centimeters) per year (about the same rate as your fingernails grow). When plates move, a gap, or space, can form. This gap is called a fault. Most earthquakes occur along faults, making the ground seem to shake and quake. In 1906, a fault that developed where two plates meet in California caused the great San Francisco earthquake.

The Blue Planet

Earth is the only planet with liquid water on its surface. In fact, most of Earth's surface— 71 percent—is covered by water. All of this water makes Earth look blue from space. For this reason, it is sometimes called the blue planet. If Earth didn't have so much

Earth looks blue from space because it has so much water.

water, people wouldn't be able to survive.

Water also affects Earth's temperature. Earth has a mild average surface temperature

Water helps make life possible on Earth.

of 59 degrees Fahrenheit (15 degrees Celsius). The oceans help to keep the temperature from being too cold in winter and too hot in summer.

A Look Inside

We know what Earth looks like on the surface because we can see it. Scientists, however, are not able to travel 4,000 miles (6,440 km) to Earth's center to see what it looks like there. Instead, they use special instruments that give them clues about the

We can study the atmosphere and surface of Earth because they are right outside. But we need special instruments to see deep inside the planet.

inside of Earth. Scientists believe Earth has four main layers.

The first layer, the crust, covers the surface of the Earth. It is made of a rocky

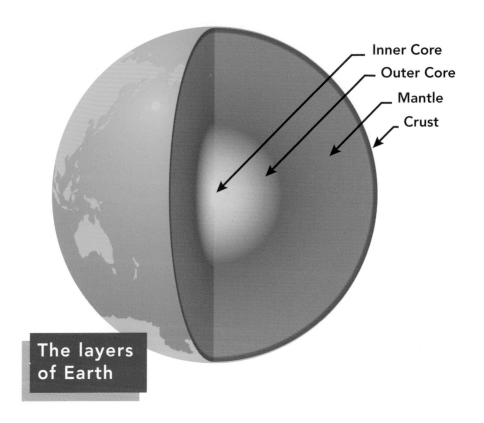

Inner Core
Outer Core
Mantle
Crust

The layers of Earth

material that is thicker beneath the continents and thinner under the oceans. The crust is the coolest part of our planet. Beneath the crust lies the mantle, a layer that is about

1,800 miles (2,900 km) thick.
Most of the mantle is solid
rock. But scientists think the
part closest to the crust is
made up of rock that is soft
enough to squeeze—like tooth-
paste in a tube. Sometimes this
hot, soft rock, called magma,
flows into cracks in the crust.
When magma flows out of the
Earth through a volcano, it is
called lava.

The third layer of Earth is
called the outer core. It is

about 1,300 miles (2,100 km) thick and consists of a hot liquid made up of iron and nickel. Temperatures at the very deepest level of the outer core can reach 9,000°F (5,000°C). That's almost as hot as the surface of the Sun!

At the very center is the inner core. Scientists think it is a solid ball of iron and nickel that floats within the liquid outer core. Temperatures here reach 11,000°F (6,100°C).

The Moon

The Moon is Earth's only natural satellite (an object that orbits around a planet). Many artificial satellites, or spacecraft, have been placed in orbit around Earth. Scientists use them to study our planet.

The Moon is an average of 238,700 miles (384,000 km)

Artificial satellites orbit around Earth.

from Earth. It is Earth's closest neighbor in the solar system. More spacecraft have been sent to the Moon than to any other object in space. The first of these was *Luna 2* (Soviet Union) in 1959.

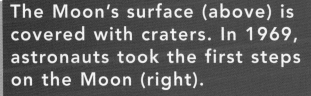

The Moon's surface (above) is covered with craters. In 1969, astronauts took the first steps on the Moon (right).

So far, the Moon is the only object in space that has been visited by people. In July 1969, the U.S. spacecraft *Apollo 11* was launched to the Moon.

The Eagle Has Landed

The goal of the Apollo flights was to land people on the Moon and bring them safely back to Earth. *Apollo 11* was the first spacecraft to reach that goal.

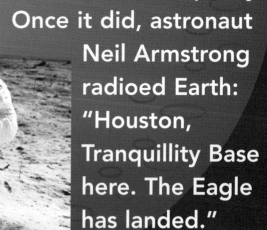

Apollo 11's lander *Eagle* touched down on the Moon's surface on July 20, 1969, after a four-day journey from Earth. It landed in a dusty part of the Moon called the Sea of Tranquillity. Once it did, astronaut Neil Armstrong radioed Earth: "Houston, Tranquillity Base here. The Eagle has landed."

Astronaut Neil Armstrong took the first-ever steps on its surface.

The *Lunar Prospector,* the United States's first moon mission in twenty-five years, was launched in January 1998 to orbit the Moon. In March 1998, it sent back information that showed there might be water ice at both of the Moon's poles. The *Lunar Prospector* will continue to collect information about this important discovery.

Earth's Future

Earth's atmosphere has just the right mix of gases for people to breathe. The oceans and the atmosphere help keep Earth at a comfortable temperature for human life. The atmosphere also keeps harmful meteoroids (pieces of rock from

The atmosphere can't keep out all meteoroids. This crater in Arizona was made by a meteorite long ago.

space) from crashing into our planet.

For thousands of years, Earth has had all that we need to survive. But that may change. If the gases in the atmosphere change too much, Earth may no longer be able to protect us and provide for us.

Scientists have begun to see changes. Earth's atmosphere now contains more carbon dioxide than it did

Cars let off a lot of carbon dioxide into the atmosphere.

one hundred years ago.
This is probably because so many people drive cars and burn coal and wood. Burning trees means fewer forests, which means fewer plants to produce much-needed oxygen.

Because of these changes, scientists think Earth is getting hotter. Perhaps Earth is warning us to take better care of the third planet from the Sun.

Earth is the only planet known to support life—and we need to take good care of our home.

Earth Quick Facts

Diameter	7,973 miles (12,756 km)
Average distance from the Sun	93 million miles (150 million km)
Average surface temperature	59°F (15°C)
Length of day	23.9345 hours
Length of year	365.256 days
Moons	1

Some Missions to the Moon

Mission	Launch Date
Luna 2 (Soviet Union)	September 1959
Luna 9 (Soviet Union)	February 1966
Apollo 11 (USA)	July 1969
Apollo 12 (USA)	November 1969
Luna 16 (Soviet Union)	September 1970
Apollo 14 (USA)	January 1971
Apollo 15 (USA)	July 1971
Apollo 16 (USA)	April 1972
Apollo 17 (USA)	December 1972
Lunar Prospector (USA)	January 1998

To Find Out More

Here are more places to learn about Earth and other planets in space:

 **Books**

Gibbons, Gail. **Planet Earth/Inside Out**. Morrow Junior Books, 1995.

Lauber, Patricia. **You're Aboard Spaceship Earth.** HarperCollins Publishers, 1996.

Planet Earth. Oxford University Press, 1993.

Sattler, Helen Roney. **Our Patchwork Planet.** Lothrop, Lee & Shepard Books, 1995.

Van Rose, Susanna. **Eyewitness Science: Earth.** DK Publishing, Inc., 1994.

Organizations and Online Sites

The Children's Museum of Indianapolis

3000 N. Meridian Street
Indianapolis, IN 46208-4716
(317) 924-5431
*http://childrensmuseum.
org/sq1.htm*

Visit the SpaceQuest Planetarium to see what it has to offer, including a view of this month's night sky.

National Aeronautics and Space Administration (NASA)

http://www.nasa.gov

At NASA's home page, you can access information about its exciting history and present resources and missions.

National Air and Space Museum

Smithsonian Institution
601 Independence Ave. SW
Washington, DC 20560
(202) 357-1300
http://www.nasm.si.edu/

The National Air and Space Museum site gives you up-to-date information about its programs and exhibits.

The Nine Planets

*http://seds.lpl.arizona.edu/
nineplanets/nineplanets/*

Take a multimedia tour of the solar system and all its planets and moons.

Space Telescope Science Institute

3700 San Martin Drive
Johns Hopkins University
Homewood Campus
Baltimore, MD 21218
(410) 338-4700
http://www.stsci.edu//

The Space Telescope Science Institute operates the Hubble Space Telescope. Visit this site to see pictures of the telescope's outer-space view.

Windows to the Universe

*http://windows.engin.
umich.edu/*

This site lets you click on all nine planets to find information about each one. It also covers many other space subjects, including important historical figures, scientists, and astronauts.

45

Important Words

atmosphere the gases that surround a planet

elliptical shaped like a stretched-out circle

fault a gap that forms when two plates move away from one another

meteoroid a fragment, or piece, of rock from space. It is called a meteorite when it strikes a planet's surface.

orbit to travel around an object

plates pieces of Earth's crust that move slowly and constantly

rotate to spin

satellite any object that orbits around a planet

solar system a group of planets and other objects that orbit around a star, such as our Sun

Index

Meet the Author

Larry Dane Brimner is the author of more than fifty books for young readers, including these other titles in the True Book series: *E-mail, The World Wide Web,* and *The Winter Olympics.* He lives with his dog, Buddy, in San Diego, California, where they often walk beneath Earth's Moon.